SACRAMENTO PUBLIC LIBRARY
828 "I" Street
Sacra to, CA 95814
/20

D0821019

UNSUNG HEROES
of Hispanic Heritage

MARIO MOLINA

NOBEL PRIZE-WINNING CHEMIST

Tammy Gagne

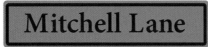

PUBLISHERS

2001 SW 31st Avenue
Hallandale, FL 33009
www.mitchelllane.com

Copyright © 2021 by Mitchell Lane Publishers. All rights reserved. No part of this book may be reproduced without written permission from the publisher. Printed and bound in the United States of America.

First Edition, 2021.
Author: Tammy Gagne
Designer: Ed Morgan
Editor: Morgan Brody

Series: Unsung Heroes of Hispanic Heritage
Title: Mario Molina: Nobel Prize-Winning Chemist / by Tammy Gagne

Hallandale, FL : Mitchell Lane Publishers, [2021]

Library bound ISBN: 978-1-68020-675-3
eBook ISBN: 978-1-68020-676-0

PHOTO CREDITS: Design Elements, freepik.com, cover: Esteban Cobo/EFE/Newscom, p 5 Shutterstock, p. 6 Associated Press, p. 9 Associated Press, p. 11 Shutterstock, p. 12 Shutterstock, p. 13 Shutterstock, p. 15 Album / J.Enrique Molina/Newscom, p. 17 GDA Photo Service/ Newscom, p. 19 German Federal Archives, p. 21 LUIS CORTES GDA Photo Service/Newscom, p. 23 Associated Press, p. 27 RAMIRO MOLINA Notimex/Newscom, p. 31 AFLO Sports/Newscom, p. 33 INNA BIGUN/SCIENCE PHOTO LIBRARY/Newscom, p. 35 JOSE PAZOS F./NOTIMEX/ Newscom, p. 37 Associated Press, p. 39 Shutterstock, p. 41 Pete Souza/The White House / PSG/Newscom, p. 43 KEVIN DIETSCH/UPI/Newscom

CONTENTS

MAKING A DIFFERENCE

"Now," the teacher said, **"we will hear from Alicia Ramirez."** Alicia took a deep breath as she gathered the notecards on her desk. She headed towards the front of the classroom with an equal mix of terror and excitement. Public speaking made her nervous, but Alicia loved talking about science. It had been her favorite subject since she first learned about the hole in the Earth's ozone layer. The ozone layer is part of the Earth's atmosphere. It protects the planet from the sun's dangerous radiation. Without the ozone layer, life could not survive on the planet.

Mario Molina was one of the first scientists to warn
the world about the hole in Earth's ozone layer.

"I chose Mario Molina for my oral report," Alicia
told her classmates. "In 1995, he received the Nobel
Prize for Chemistry. He won the award for his research
about the ozone hole over Antarctica." She then
explained that the hole in the ozone layer affects other
continents as well. It allows dangerous ultraviolet rays
from the sun to reach the earth. "These UVB rays
cause skin cancer and other health problems. They also
hurt natural ecosystems," she added.

Alicia had been practicing how to pronounce the word *chlorofluorocarbons* for days. Just to be safe, though, she had written it like it sounded on her note card. "Mario Molina was the first person to realize that chemicals called klor-oh-flur-oh-car-buns, or CFCs, destroy ozone. These gases are used to make refrigerators, plastic foams, aerosol sprays, and other products." Alicia set her notes down and exhaled. The hard part was over. Now she could focus on just speaking about the man she so admired.

"Molina made his discovery in 1973. At first many people did not listen to him. Perhaps they didn't believe him. Or maybe they just didn't want to believe him. After all, the products containing the CFCs made life easier for many people. The companies that manufactured these products also made lots of money from them. Some worried that finding other ways to make them would be expensive. But the cost of destroying the ozone layer would be much greater." Alicia paused a moment for effect. Like many people, she believed that protecting the environment was of utmost importance. "Although it would take many years, Molina's theory would eventually be proven correct. His research eventually helped change many environmental policies all over the world. Now, it is up to us to stop destroying this important part of our atmosphere."

The assignment had been to select someone who had made an important contribution to science and tell the class about it. The teacher told the students they could choose any person they wanted. But for Alicia, no one else even came close. Molina came from the same part of Mexico as her grandparents. She was proud to share her heritage—and a love of science—with him. He was the first Mexican-born person to win a Nobel Prize for Chemistry. The award was also the first Nobel Prize awarded for work relating to the environment. Alicia planned to become a scientist when she grew up. Her biggest dream was to fix the ozone layer.

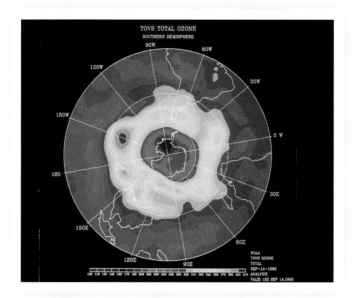

The ozone hole over Antarctica is shown in the center of the image.

WINNING THE NOBEL PRIZE

Molina shared the Nobel Prize for Chemistry with fellow chemists F. Sherwood Rowland and Paul Crutzen. Molina and Rowland worked together at the University of California at Berkeley. Crutzen performed his own research in Germany. His work focused on nitrogen oxide and its damage to the ozone layer.

CHAPTER TWO

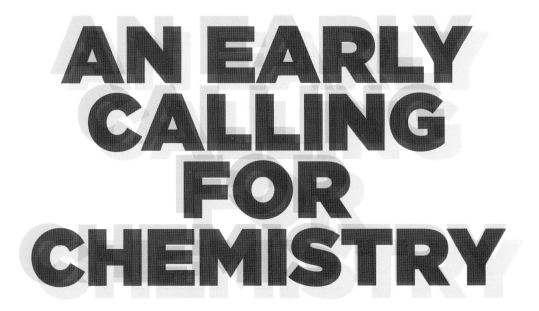

AN EARLY CALLING FOR CHEMISTRY

On March 19, 1943, Leonor Henriquez de Molina and her husband Roberto Molina Pasquel welcomed a baby boy. The couple named their new son Mario José Molina. The family lived in Mexico City, the capital of Mexico. Mario's father was a lawyer. He also served as a Mexican diplomat to Australia, Ethiopia, and the Philippines. A diplomat is a person works as a peacemaker between one country and another. Mario did not want to be either a lawyer or a diplomat, though. He was drawn to science.

Mario loved learning about science even as a little boy. He enjoyed hands-on activities about science. As an adult, he still recalls how excited he got looking at slides with his toy microscope. This was his introduction to single-celled animals called paramecia and amoebae. But he already wanted to learn more. He asked his parents if he could turn an extra bathroom in their home into his own laboratory. He spent hours in the makeshift space playing with toy chemistry sets.

Mario's aunt, Esther Molina, was a chemist. Like his parents, she encouraged his deep interest in science. When Mario quickly outgrew the kinds of experiments other kids his age were doing, she helped him conduct more challenging tests in his lab. These experiments were closer to the work of chemistry students in college. Mario's own classmates did not share his passion for chemistry. They also could not keep up with his strong understanding of the subject.

The early experiments Mario conducted as a child laid the groundwork for his future career in chemistry.

When he was 11, Mario's parents decided to send him to boarding school in Switzerland. There, he could study chemistry at a level that better matched his abilities. He could also learn German. His parents knew this language was an important one for a chemist. Many of the greatest chemists in the world spoke and wrote in this language. Years later, Molina wrote about his early life on the Nobel Prize website, "I remember I was thrilled to go to Europe, but then I was disappointed in that my European schoolmates had no more interest in science than my Mexican friends."

Of course, science wasn't young Mario's only interest. He was also a talented violinist. For a while he even thought about making his living in some way with music. But chemistry won out. When the time came to head to college, Mario returned to Mexico. He enrolled at the National Autonomous University of Mexico as a chemical engineering major in 1960. It was the closest program he could find that would set him on the path of becoming a research chemist. He graduated in 1965 with a bachelor's degree.

Mario enrolled in the National Autonomous University of Mexico
to earn his bachelor's degree in chemical engineering.

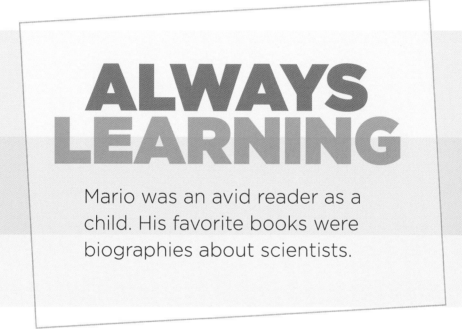

ALWAYS LEARNING

Mario was an avid reader as a child. His favorite books were biographies about scientists.

Little did young Mario imagine as a child that one day students would be reading stories about his life and work.

CHAPTER THREE

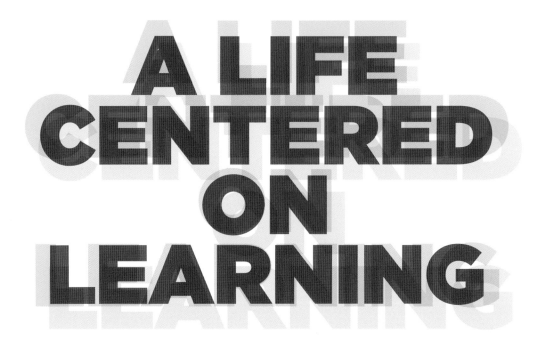

A LIFE CENTERED ON LEARNING

University of Freiburg in the 1960s

Molina's chemical engineering degree was a good first step in his secondary education. But it was just one step. After earning his bachelor's, Molina decided to work towards an advanced degree in physical chemistry. All the German that he had learned during his boarding school days was also about to pay off. He enrolled at the University of Freiburg in Germany. He knew he still had much to learn in the areas of mathematics and physics. Molina spent the next two years doing research in kinetics of polymerizations. This area of study deals with the chemical nature of plastics. He added the equivalent of a master's degree from the university to his résumé in 1967.

Molina had spent years of his life studying science. And he wasn't finished yet. But for now it was time to enjoy some other experiences. He traveled to Paris for some time away from school. While in France's capital city, Molina made several good friends. They spent time discussing topics relating to the arts, philosophy, and politics. He was looking at the world in completely new ways. These few months away from his formal education did not keep him from his plan, though. He was still determined to become a research chemist.

When Molina returned to Mexico, he once again headed to the National Autonomous University of Mexico. This time the school hired him as an assistant professor. When he had been a student, the university did not offer anything beyond a bachelor's degree in chemical engineering. Molina decided to start a graduate program for students who wanted to go further in this field.

Although Molina had a wide range of interests, he never lost sight of his goal to become a research chemist.

Soon, though, it was time for him to finish his education. In 1968, Molina traveled outside Mexico yet again. This time he went to the University of California at Berkeley to complete his own graduate studies. He received his Ph.D. from the school in 1972. The following year, he moved to the school's campus in Irvine to conduct research about atmospheric chemistry.

It was around this time that he began working with a man by the name of F. Sherwood Rowland. His friends called him Sherry. Together, Molina and Rowland formed a theory about chlorofluorocarbons and their effect on the atmosphere. They called it the CFC-Ozone Depletion Theory. Evidence they collected from their research showed that human-made chemicals were damaging the Earth's ozone layer. This prompted them to try to find a way to destroy the CFCs before they could rise high enough to harm this important part of Earth's atmosphere. If it could not be done, then something had to be done to stop companies from using these chemicals.

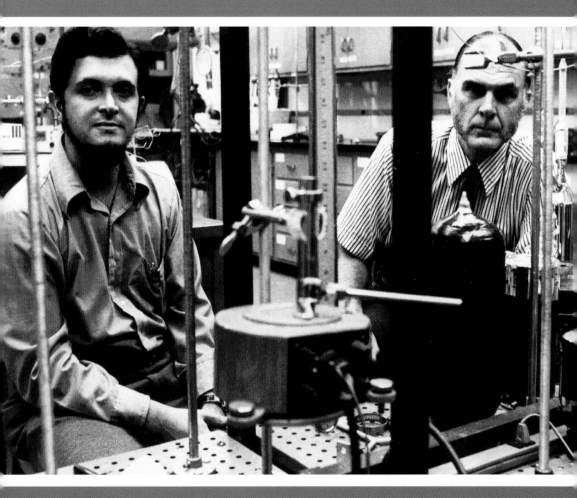

Molina and Rowland worked hard to find a solution to the
problem of the depleting ozone layer.

In their paper, Molina and Rowland pointed out that the problem was only going to get worse. "These compounds are chemically inert and may remain in the atmosphere for 40–150 years, and concentrations can be expected to reach 10 to 30 times present levels."

A look at the many parts of Earth's atmosphere.

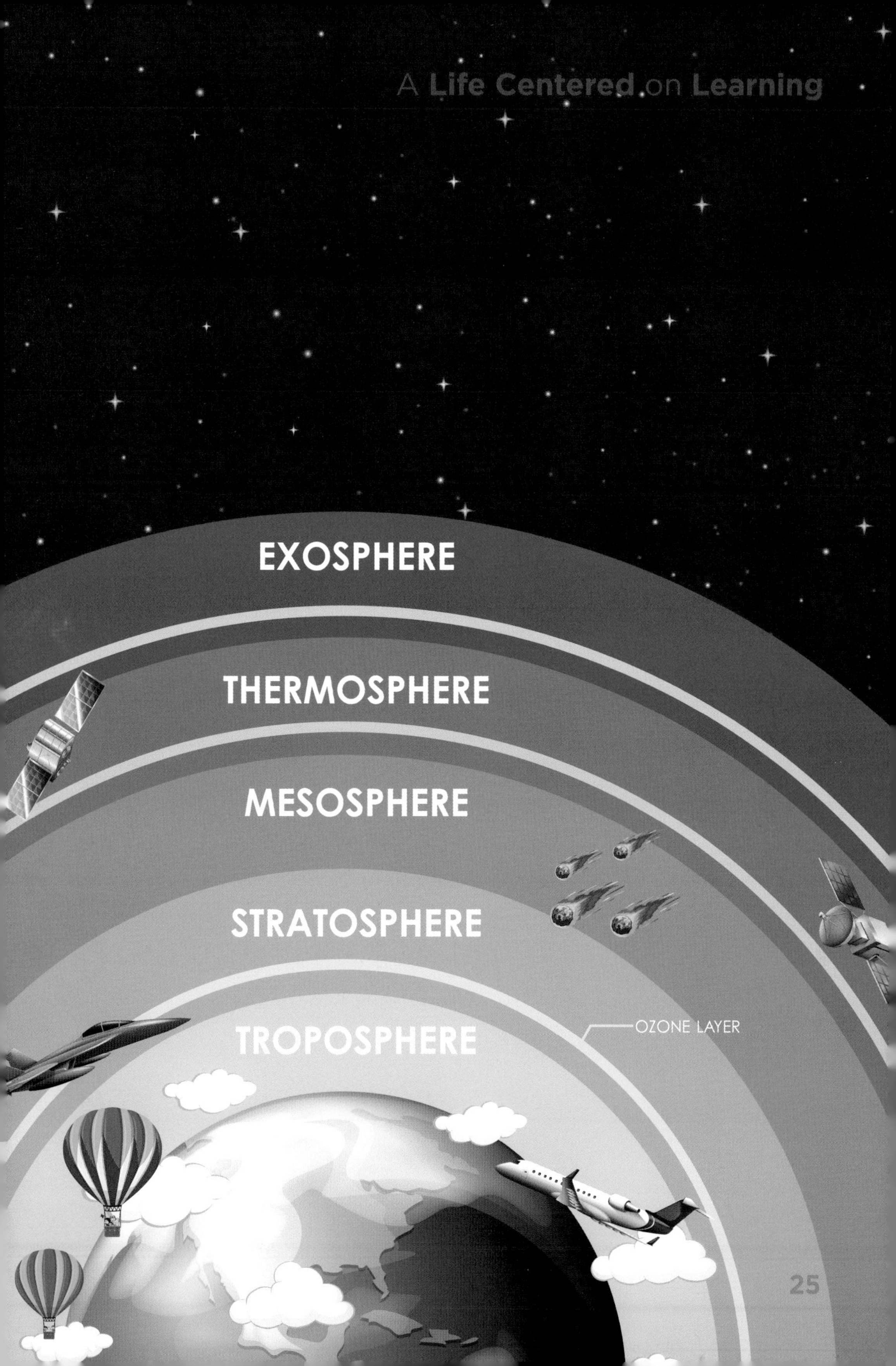

EXOSPHERE

THERMOSPHERE

MESOSPHERE

STRATOSPHERE

TROPOSPHERE

OZONE LAYER

25

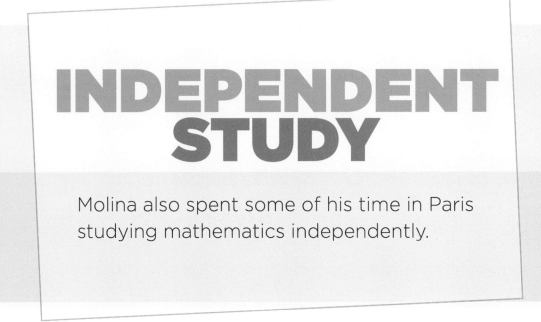

INDEPENDENT STUDY

Molina also spent some of his time in Paris studying mathematics independently.

Molina has received more than forty honorary degrees, such as this one from the University of the America in 2001, during his lifetime.

CHAPTER FOUR

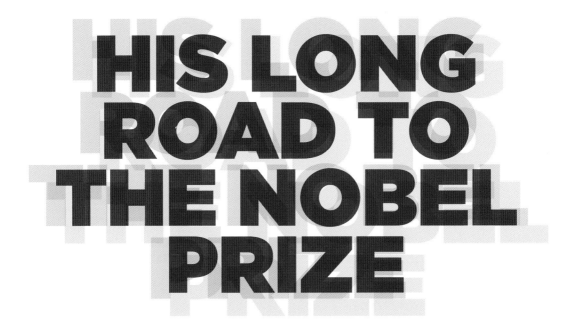

HIS LONG ROAD TO THE NOBEL PRIZE

Molina and Rowland shared their theory about CFCs with the public in 1974. Many industrial businesses that made or used CFCs quickly became defensive. After all, manufacturing CFCs brought in a whopping $2 billion a year. This was no small amount of money, especially in the 1970s. The companies responded by attacking the theory and the men who were sharing it with the world.

Many politicians also immediately dismissed the possibility that the scientists were right. The idea that human activities had an impact on the environment was a new concept at this time. People were used to doing things certain ways. Many of them were unwilling to change their habits because of a new theory, regardless of the evidence presented with it.

Molina and Rowland suspected they were onto something after making an important comparison in their lab. First, they looked at the total amount of CFCs that had been measured in the Earth's atmosphere. Next, they looked at the amount of the same gases that industrial companies around the world had emitted. The two figures were about the same, which led the scientists to their initial hypothesis: The gases that were being released were not breaking down like many other types of gases did. Instead, they were staying in the environment for as long as a century. Soon Molina and Rowland also discovered that these gases were affecting the ozone layer. They concluded that these chemicals would create even greater damage if industry kept releasing them.

Molina and Rowland did not let the naysayers stop them. They stood by their work. They knew it was important to share their discovery with the rest of the world. In an interview with the *New York Times*, Rowland stated that people within the scientific community acknowledged that the theory made sense. "[R]ight from the beginning, people were saying, 'It sounds bizarre, but all the steps are plausible.'"

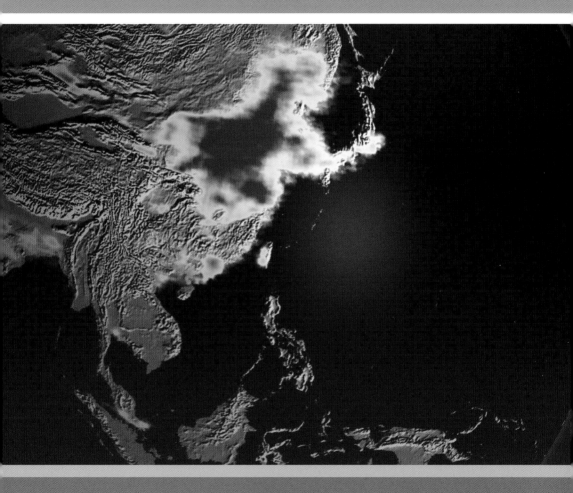

Some types of chemical pollution can be seen over
the areas where they are most common.

It took time for other scientists to back up Molina and Rowland's theory. By 1985, though, the problem had become an even bigger one. Environmental scientists discovered that the ozone layer above Antarctica was especially thin. It had become so thin in fact that many scientists began referring to it as a hole. A Dutch chemist named Paul Crutzen was able to link the thinning ozone with chemical reactions that were taking place in the clouds above the continent. Two years later, an international agreement was made to lower CFC use globally. It was called the Montreal Protocol.

The work and persistence of these three chemists had made a remarkable difference for the planet and all its inhabitants. Before, no one had even been aware of the problem CFCs were causing in the environment. Now, companies around the globe were working together to protect the Earth by lessening their use. The three men were awarded the 1995 Nobel Prize for Chemistry for their pioneering work.

The ozone layer protects all types of life on the planet.

PUBLISHED WORK

Molina and Rowland published their findings about CFCs in a British journal called *Nature*. Their paper appeared in the June 28, 1974 issue.

Molina had always wanted to do important work as a research chemist. His discovery of the ozone hole was just that.

— CHAPTER FIVE —

FURTHER RESEARCH

Molina and his fellow 1995 Nobel Prize recipients for Chemistry, F. Sherwood Rowland (*left*) and Paul Crutzen (*right*).

In the years following their CFC-Ozone Depletion Theory, Molina and Rowland remained good friends. But they stopped working together. Rowland was 16 years older than Molina. He was already an experienced research chemist when the two began working together. But Molina was just getting started as a researcher. Like many young people, he felt he had to prove himself.

In 1975, he began teaching at the University of California. He began as an assistant professor and was later promoted to an associate professor. But his heart still resided in the laboratory. He liked teaching, but he missed performing his own experiments. In 1982, he moved to the Jet Propulsion Laboratory. He was overjoyed to be working with his own two hands again. His work continued to relate to the atmosphere.

By 1989, though, it was time for another change. This one would take him across the country to Boston. It also brought him back to academics with a position at the Massachusetts Institute of Technology (MIT). There, he came to realize that teaching and researching go hand in hand.

While teaching at MIT, Molina realized that educating others would always be an important part of his career in environmental chemistry.

After working in the United States for a while, Molina decided to become a naturalized U.S. citizen. Doing so made it possible for him to work in the country's national labs. It also helped him effect more change in U.S. policies on the environment. He even served on the U.S. President's Council of Advisors on Science and Technology during the Obama administration. Molina's work made a profound difference in slowing down the damage to the ozone layer. In 1996, the United States banned CFCs. Many other nations followed suit.

Molina has also helped other people interested in saving the environment through chemistry research. He donated nearly all the money from his Nobel Prize to scientists and educators in developing nations. He knew they sorely lacked the funds needed for their own research. After leaving MIT in 2005, Molina also returned to Mexico City. He created a research center there so other scientists from his native country could also make an impact to environmental chemistry. During an interview with the National Autonomous University of Mexico, Molina explained, "Science is a great means of unification for the peoples of the world."

Molina was able to help shape governmental policy on environmental issues by serving on President Obama's Council of Advisors on Science and Technology.

HONORING HIS SERVICE

In 2013, President Barack Obama awarded Mario Molina with the U.S. Presidential Medal of Freedom. This is the highest honor that the United States awards civilians.

During the ceremony, President Obama said that Molina's work has inspired others to work toward leaving the planet a safer place for future generations.

TIMELINE

TIMELINE TIMELINE

1943   Mario Molina is born in Mexico City, Mexico on March 19.

1965   He graduates from the National Autonomous University of Mexico with a bachelor's degree in chemical engineering.

1967   He receives the equivalent of a master's degree in physical chemistry from Germany's University of Freiburg.

1972   Molina receives his Ph.D. at the University of California, Berkeley.

1973   He discovered that chlorofluorocarbons are causing great damage to the Earth's ozone layer.

1974   Molina and F. Sherwood Rowland present their CFC-Ozone Depletion Theory in an article in the British journal, *Nature*.

1995   Molina and Rowland, along with Dutch chemist Paul Crutzen, are awarded the Nobel Prize for Chemistry.

2013   President Barack Obama awards Molina the Presidential Medal of Freedom.

FIND OUT MORE

Chastain, Zachary. *How Do Industrial Chemicals Affect Your Health?* Vestal, NY: Village Earth Press, 2016.

Heinecke, Liz Lee. *Kitchen Science Lab for Kids*. Beverly, MA: Quarry Books, 2019.

Kiddle. Mario Molina facts for kids. https://kids.kiddle.co/Mario_J._Molina

National Geographic Society. Ozone layer. https://www.nationalgeographic.org/encyclopedia/ozone-layer/

Rusch, Elizabeth. *Mario and the Hole in the Sky*. Watertown, MA: Charlesbridge, 2019.

Sciencing. What Are the Sources of CFCs? https://sciencing.com/sources-cfcs-8405334.html

WORKS CONSULTED

_____. "Health and Environmental Effects of Ozone Layer Depletion." United States Environmental Protection Agency. https://www.epa.gov/ozone-layer-protection/health-and-environmental-effects-ozone-layer-depletion

_____. "Chlorofluorocarbons." U.S. National Library of Medicine. https://toxtown.nlm.nih.gov/chemicals-and-contaminants/chlorofluorocarbons-cfcs

_____. "Mario J. Molina" The Nobel Prize. https://www.nobelprize.org/prizes/chemistry/1995/molina/biographical/

_____. "Mario J. Molina: Interview." The Nobel Prize. https://www.nobelprize.org/prizes/chemistry/1995/molina/interview/

_____. "Mario Molina." American Institute of Physics. https://history.aip.org/phn/11806011.html

_____. "Mario Molina." Encyclopedia Britannica. https://www.britannica.com/biography/Mario-Molina

_____. "Mario Molina." Science History Institute. https://www.sciencehistory.org/historical-profile/mario-molina

_____. "Paul Crutzen." Encyclopedia Britannica. https://www.britannica.com/biography/Paul-Crutzen

Davidson, Jean. "Ozone Issue Expert Says Don't Wait to Ban CFCs." *Los Angeles Times*, March 4, 1989. https://www.latimes.com/archives/la-xpm-1989-03-04-me-284-story.html

Denmark, Bonnie. "Mario Molina: Atmospheric Chemistry to Change Global Policy." Visionlearning, 2015. https://www.visionlearning.com/en/library/Inside-Science/58/Mario-Molina/211

Molina, Mario J. and Rowland, F.S. "Stratospheric sink for chlorofluoromethanes: chlorine atom-catalysed destruction of ozone." *Nature*, June 28, 1974. https://www.nature.com/articles/249810a0

Soloman, Susan. "Mario Molina." Science History Institute. December 12, 2017. https://www.sciencehistory.org/historical-profile/mario-molina

Stevens, William K. "3 Win Nobel Prize for Work on Threat to Ozone." *The New York Times*, October 12, 1995. https://www.nytimes.com/1995/10/12/us/3-win-nobel-prize-for-work-on-threat-to-ozone.html

INDEX

ABOUT THE AUTHOR

Tammy Gagne has written more than 200 books for both adults and children. Among her favorites have been titles about people from different cultures with great passion for their life and work. *Mario Molina* is one such book. Others include *Juan Felipe Herrera* and *Sylvia Mendez*.